MW01593736

101 Leadership Actions

for

Effective Presentations

OLLIE MALONE, PH.D.

HRD Press • Amherst • Massachusetts

Published by:

HRD Press
22 Amherst Road
Amherst, MA 01002
1-800-822-2801 (U.S. and Canada)
413-253-3488
413-253-3490 (FAX)
www.hrdpress.com

ISBN 0-87425-803-0

Cover design by Perri Harper
Editorial services by Sally Farnham
Production services by PerfecType

Table of Contents

Curtain Up!

The projector is on. The room is full. Your introduction is about finished. You're about to be called to the lectern. Now what?

Throughout the world, countless leaders are making presentations at any given day of the week.

Are you one of them?

This book is based on our experience of training thousands of individuals in giving effective presentations. These individuals have gone on to give presentations in academic environments, sales settings, political settings, religious environments, and face-to-face interactions.

According to numerous surveys, people dread giving presentations. In fact, the dreading is right up there with death and taxes.

We believe that "presentation-dread" is a curable disease and we have formulated this book as the medicine for that cure. Like all medicines, however, possession alone is not the solution. We recommend that you read it regularly and put the many ideas here to practice. They've already been tested with others—you just need to pick the ones that will work for you. Break a leg!

Getting the Most Out of This Book...

This book is organized in such a way that you need not read it from cover to cover. In fact, you might be a bit bored reading the entire book, and doing so will not necessarily provide you with the greatest benefit.

Our recommendation is this:

- Use this book as a handbook by laying it side-by-side with the presentation you may be currently working on.
- As you encounter a snag in your presentation efforts or simply want some new ideas, check the book.
- After you've finished your presentation, review some of the suggestions in this book for moving beyond your initial organization into the refining and polishing phase of your presentation.

- Get a copy of this book for those who work with you or those who may need some fresh suggestions for better impacting the audiences to whom they speak.

As you become more skillful in delivering presentations, use this book as a diary; jot down other suggestions in the margins of the book that you have found to be particularly helpful.

Your listeners won't know what hit them!

Start with a
Brain Transplant

Many people struggle with delivering effective presentations because their assumptions about presentations are faulty in nature. In the list below, check the box next to each statement that reflects your views about developing and delivering presentations.

- ☐ Giving presentations is a necessary evil.
- ☐ I wouldn't deliver presentations if I didn't have to.
- ☐ Some days I'm better at presenting information than others.
- ☐ I just don't have "the gift of gab."
- ☐ I just can't stand up and "b___ s___" my way through minutes of worthless rhetoric. I'm a "just the facts" kind of person.

☐ Giving a presentation is an opportunity for me to impress people with what I know about a given topic.

☐ I believe I know a lot about this topic, and I am looking forward to an opportunity to share some of that knowledge with others.

☐ I see myself becoming more effective at delivering presentations with every one that I do.

If you checked any one of the first six boxes, it may be time for you to reconsider your beliefs about your presentations. As you do and begin to adopt some of the beliefs and assumptions reflected in the last two, you'll enjoy presentations more—and you'll likely find that you're better at them.

Give it a try!

1

Start to see yourself as the world's best presenter.

For many, the problem of effective presentations begins with a wrong self-image. They see themselves as clumsy, awkward, ill-at-ease, and then— voilà—they are. Start training your brain to see yourself not as a failure, but as a wildly successful person. Take note of how you look, how you feel, and what you're doing. Keep those images alive; they will serve you well as you move closer to the image.

2

Make a list of those things you would be doing.

There are certain things the greatest presenters do that the not-so-great presenters do not do. What do you see the "top-shelf" presenters do? How do they connect with you? How are their materials presented? How do they connect with other members of the audience? Learn from those who are really excellent—and borrow their ideas liberally.

3

Make a list of words and/or terms that describe "the new you."

Your list should not resemble *War and Peace,* but rather should be five to seven words/terms that capture either how you would like to feel on the inside or how you would like to be seen by others. Your list might include the following: Ease, engaging, knowledgeable, and worth listening to.

4

Find out what others like about your presentations.

Sometimes we're our own worst critics when it comes to presentations, yet others are able to see the strengths that often elude us. Get some feedback from others: What do they see you doing well? Write down their positive comments—and capitalize on them.

5

Continue to refine your "new you" list.

As you hear other words or terms that you would like to be applied to you, add them to the list formed in #3 above. Make this list a dynamic part of your preparation to present. Sharpen your descriptions, where necessary, and eliminate those that no longer work for you. Remember to keep your list at a manageable five to seven descriptors.

6

Ask others what they'd like to see you do differently.

This might be difficult, but try *not* to think of it as a report card. This is a way for you to identify the "outer limits" of your presentation behavior. In other words, the lists you generated in #3 and #4 above represent the positive side of presentations for you. This is the negative side and forms a boundary for you. If you think your presentation is swaying toward this boundary, turn around!

7

Make yourself a student of effective presentations.

Most of us are in situations where we frequently see and hear others make presentations. It might be something you observe on the television, a business or professional meeting you attend, or a religious service: Notice not only what is being said, but how it is being said. The "how" is another resource for you in your presentation-improvement strategy.

8

Ask others about their perspectives on effective presentations.

By now, you've probably figured out that one of the most important things about presentations and their effectiveness is the mind-set that you bring to those presentations. If you've gotten that message, good job! Ask others what their perspectives are on effective presentations. Doing so should help you think about your presentations differently.

9

Get yourself "grounded" for your presentation.

We'll explore this further in later sections, but our observation of those who struggle with presentations do so because they are disconnected from themselves, they are disconnected from the earth, or they are disconnected from their audience. By "grounded" we mean "being in touch with…." As opposed to avoiding this presentation, see yourself as being well connected to it. Get grounded!

10

Work in a way that supports your best results.

As you begin the process of building a successful presentation, bear in mind who you are: your strengths, your weaknesses, those things you do well, those things you do not, and those things you are working to improve. As you build a world-class presentation, keep these personal characteristics in mind. Your presentation development could hold significant opportunities for your continued growth and development. Don't miss out!

Prepare Thoroughly

Whether you're a seasoned presenter looking for a few presentation pointers or you're a rank novice, preparation is one of the keys to your success.

What are your attitudes about preparation? In the list below, check the box next to each statement that pertains to you.

- ☐ Preparing for a presentation is a necessary evil.
- ☐ I wouldn't prepare for a presentation if I didn't have to.
- ☐ Some days I'm better at presentation preparation than others.
- ☐ I just don't think that way.
- ☐ I can stand up and "b___ s___" my way through minutes of worthless rhetoric. I guess I should have been a comedian.

☐ This is an opportunity for me to impress people with what I already know about a given topic.

☐ I am looking forward to preparing well so that I can effectively share some of my knowledge with others.

☐ I see myself becoming more effective at preparing presentations with every one that I do.

If you checked any one of the first six boxes, it may be time for you to reconsider your beliefs about your presentations. As you do and begin to adopt some of the beliefs and assumptions reflected in the last two, you'll enjoy presentations more—and you'll likely find that you're better at them. So, sharpen your pencil and let's get started.

11

Understand your presentation's purpose(s).

Most people do not present for the "sport" of it. They usually have some larger purpose or desired outcome for their presentations. These desired outcomes could include: informing the audience, making a sale, obtaining support, solving a problem, or gaining support for an idea.

12

Identify and write down your purpose.

The purpose of your presentation will significantly affect both the way you organize and the way you deliver your presentation. Get crystal clear about the purpose of your presentation and once you have done so, write it down. In fact, you may want to write down several and review these either individually or with some other person to ensure that your purpose is, indeed, on-point

13

Review your preparation against your purpose.

It is rather pointless to have a purpose if your presentation content bears no resemblance to it. After you've identified the purpose for your presentation, check out your outline, activities, questions, illustrations, graphics, and other presentation-related factors against this purpose.

14

Review what you learned about outlining.

Most people, at one time or another, have learned something about outlining. It might have been in sixth-grade Reading class, or it might have been in an upper-level educational setting where it was necessary for you to outline a research report or thesis. Whatever the source, what you learned about main ideas, supporting ideas, and subordinate ideas is relevant to your preparation.

15

Identify the main idea of your presentation.

Your main idea might be as general as "Join our professional organization," or it might be as detailed as "The 12 primary reasons for expanding, not contracting out, our commitment to space travel." Think of this main idea as the punch line or the bottom line.

16

Make your main idea compelling.

Although you might be totally enraptured with your main idea, what's the hook? Will it captivate others and interest them enough to pay attention to the ideas you are putting forth—or will the group collectively yawn at the things you regard as "compelling"?

17

Leverage the "audience factor" in your idea.

There's an old saying that goes, "Will it play in Peoria?" In other words, will your idea appeal to those for whom it is intended? If it will or if it has that possibility, move forward with deliberate speed. If the idea is more of a "ho-hum" issue, you might want to go back to the drawing board and continue wordsmithing until you have something with significantly greater "street value."

18

Incorporate humor into your main idea.

One of our favorite sayings is, "The scenery only changes for the lead dog." Most folks who hear that statement find it funny (unfortunately, not all do), but the statement reveals a significant truth as well. If you are able to find a humorous statement that supports your main idea, milk it for all it's worth!

19

Beta test your idea with the "man-on-the-street."

If you are able to identify an "ordinary Joe or Jane," press them into service by asking them to review your main idea and offer their comments on your main idea. If it was intended to be funny, is it? If it was supposed to be serious, is it? Test your assumptions against this individual's to determine if what you're thinking works.

20

Willingly change your main idea if necessary.

If your main idea isn't working, kill it before it multiplies! It is totally pointless for you to move forward with a lame main idea since it will only contribute to the lameness of your presentation overall. In other words, don't fall in love with your main idea. You identified this one—surely you will be able to identify another one if necessary.

21

Once you've found a great main idea, celebrate.

The identification of a main idea is a great first step in developing a winning presentation. Finding one—or developing one—is no small achievement. As the show biz tune goes, "This could be the start of something big!" Take a moment to celebrate this significant accomplishment.

22

Write down your main idea in ink.

Seal the identification of your main idea by writing it down in ink. This act symbolizes the finality of the work you've spent in achieving this milestone.

23

Identify your three to five supporting ideas.

Your supporting ideas reinforce the main idea, or they might exist to extend the main idea. In some respects, they function like punctuation in your presentation, creating pause, supplying an opportunity to reflect, establishing audience surprise, or compelling the audience to respond in a given way.

24

Make your supporting ideas compelling.

How well do your supporting ideas support your main idea? If your answer is, "I'm not so sure…" you may want to think about starting over. Refine each of your supporting ideas until they have a clear "gotcha" in them and are able to cause your audience to sit up and take notice.

25

Leverage the "audience factor" in your supporting ideas.

Similar to what was discussed in examining the main idea, your supporting ideas should be audience-focused and should be developed with your audience in mind. Similar to the work of skillful fishermen, create multiple hooks with which you can "catch" your audience.

26

Incorporate humor into your supporting ideas.

To support the notion of "The scenery only changes for the lead dog," you may want to choose a supporting idea such as, "To be the lead dog, practice running fast." This idea supports the original theme while, at the same time, continues to be funny (at least we think so).

27

Create a level of variety in your supporting ideas.

Ensure that your supporting ideas don't all sound the same. Increase audience interest by changing your supporting ideas in terms of their length, the amount of humor used in them, the level of seriousness in the ideas, or the amount of time that will be devoted to the idea.

28

Beta test your supporting ideas with the "man-on-the-street."

Just as with your main idea, identify an ordinary individual, and ask them to review your supporting ideas and provide comments on them. Follow the same process you did with your main idea to make sure your presentation works as you intend it to.

29

Willingly change your supporting ideas if necessary.

Again, just as with your main idea, don't fall in love with your supporting ideas. If they don't work they'll destroy your whole presentation.

30

Celebrate your great supporting ideas.

The identification and development of supporting ideas is as great an achievement as developing your main idea, so take another moment to give yourself a pat on the back or an "attaboy"; whatever works for you!

31

Write down your supporting ideas in ink.

In the same way that "repeaters" strengthen the signal in a signal, your supporting ideas strengthen the main idea. Their nature (humorous, serious, tragic) as well as their timing will help to strengthen your main idea and thereby reinforce your purpose. Now that you have chosen them carefully, write them down in ink—and fall in love with them.

32

Go on the hunt for data and illustrations.

Both your main ideas and your supporting ideas will take on life as you support them with data and illustrations. Your data can be statistics, anecdotes, quotations, or examples. Your illustrations can be comic strips, jokes, or stories. Just make sure these data and illustrations, whatever they are, are relevant to the point you're making (and again, you must have at least *one* point!).

33

Pick an approach for organizing your presentation.

There are several means through which presentations can be organized. There is probably no one best way for organizing your presentation other than this: Pick the approach to organization that best supports the purpose of your presentation. That's the "magic." Several organization approaches are offered in Actions 34 through 42. Use these or find others that work for you.

34

You can organize your presentation logically.

A logical approach to your presentation works particularly well if the goal of your presentation is to inform. By using a logical approach, your audience is able to follow your thought processes and, ideally, arrive at the same conclusion or outcome that you did. The obvious risk in this approach lies in the possibility of your logic containing numerous flaws. Make sure you check your logic with others before declaring it iron-clad.

35

You can organize chronologically as well.

A chronological organization to your presentation, unlike its logical counterpart, is often difficult to dispute. Here you are simply presenting facts, figures, or issues in the order of their occurrence. The one risk with this approach lies in the potential of your forgetting or leaving out (intentionally or unintentionally) facts your audience considers important.

36

Reverse chronology is another option.

Reverse chronology begins with the present and works its way backwards to the relevant past. This approach is useful as a means of addressing problems or in supporting rationale for a particular path forward. As in its chronological option, it will be important that you include all of the milestones or factors that might also be identified by your audience as important—or that you have compelling rationale for the omission of these factors.

37

The "motivated sequence" is another option.

The motivated sequence steps consist of attention, satisfaction, visualization, and action. Many television commercials use this approach to deliver a complete message in a limited period of time. Get the audience's attention, describe their need, describe how this is satisfied, give them a picture of themselves with the need satisfied, and challenge them to act. That's it.

38

Organize by dealing with history.

History, in this instance, may or may not be chronological. Your presentation could simply address a number of issues that have occurred historically, regardless of the order. This approach can be used effectively in showing how a number of historical events have an impact on current performance or current issues under consideration. As with all other fact-based organization approaches, make sure you have relevant facts included.

39

You can organize using the inverted pyramid.

The inverted pyramid puts the most important factors in your presentation first. This approach is extremely helpful when there is the possibility of your presentation time either being reduced or expanded. By focusing on the most important things first, you can be assured that if you have to cut the amount of time in your presentation, you've covered the most critical ideas that need to be addressed.

40

You can organize according to a model.

A "model" in this context is a visual representation of a thought process. For instance, if you were to describe breakdowns in your company's manufacturing process, you could help the audience visualize this by having an illustration that shows the major manufacturing tasks that occur (in the order they occur), highlighting the breakdowns as they occur in the process.

41

You can organize presentations hysterically.

When you think "hysterical organization," think about the old card game "52 Pick Up," where a deck of cards is tossed in the air and the cards are dealt with as they are picked up. This approach is a good one to keep your audience on their toes and/or to break up rigidly held assumptions about what might be true, right, or relevant.

42

You can also combine one or more approaches.

As you might imagine, some of the approaches presented here can also be easily combined to create an entirely different approach to organization. That, too, is an option for you to consider. Unless you have a level of experience in dealing with such a hybrid approach, you may want to use it judiciously. Your audience could end up leaving the presentation scratching their heads—and you with them.

43

Be willing to change your organization if needed.

Once you've chosen an approach to organization and have put it in place, you may find that it lacks something. Because several options have been presented here, there are other options that you can pursue that might be better suited to the outcomes you desire. Feel free to change. If you change, however, stick with the change. Otherwise your presentation might come off as sounding quite schizophrenic.

44

Find out whatever you can about the setting.

From a presentation standpoint, some settings are more appropriate for certain types of presentations. Is the setting a formal hotel banquet room or conference space? Are you speaking at a dude ranch? The physical setting will affect the type of presentation you develop—a more formal one, or one much less formal and much more colloquial. This will also influence your choice of examples and illustrations.

Hit the Dummy More Than Once

Although it might seem pointless, rehearsing your presentation—particularly transitions—can make the difference between a smooth-sailing vessel and the *Titanic*.

In the list below check the box next to each statement that reflects your views about rehearsing your presentation.

- ☐ Rehearsing a presentation is a necessary evil.
- ☐ I wouldn't rehearse a presentation if I didn't have to.
- ☐ Some days I actually consider rehearsing my presentation.
- ☐ I don't have "the gift of gab"—but wish I did.
- ☐ I can stand up and "b___ s___" my way through minutes of worthless rhetoric.

☐ Rehearsing my presentation is an opportunity for me to practice my spontaneity. Since I know a lot, it should be easy.

☐ I believe there is a lot I know about this topic, and I am looking forward to an opportunity to share some of that knowledge with others. Practicing might help.

☐ I see myself becoming more effective at delivering presentations with every one that I do.

If you checked any one of the first six boxes, it may be time for you to reconsider your beliefs about rehearsing. As you do and begin to adopt some of the beliefs and assumptions reflected in the last two, you'll enjoy presentations more—and your audience will likely enjoy them more also.

45

Practice in front of a mirror—a full-length one.

Other than perhaps catching a glimpse of ourselves in reflective glass, most of us have no idea how we appear to others. In this very simple practicing approach, practice a few words or sentences in front of a mirror. How do you look? Do you believe you? Do you believe others will find you credible? What should you consider doing differently?

46

Practice your presentation with an audio tape recorder.

This, too, is a challenge for most presenters in that we are not accustomed to hearing our own voices from a perspective other than the one inside our heads. Listen carefully to your voice on an audio recorder. How does it sound? Warm? Friendly? Harsh? Clipped—as if you're on your way somewhere else?

47

Make notes on what you'd like to change.

Many things about our voices are changeable—the pitch (if your voice is too high or too low), the volume (too loud or too soft), the timbre (too husky or too strident), the pace (too fast or too slow). As you listen to your voice, note those things that you'd like to be different in the audible portion of your presentation. Then practice parts of your presentation again, making the identified adjustments.

48

More than likely, you'll need to slow down!

Most presenters, when they are nervous or excited, tend to speed up the rate at which they speak. Speeding up the rate of your speech changes the meaning behind the words. If you don't believe us, try saying, "This is a great day!" fast, then slower, then at the slowest rate you can say it. As the adrenaline gets pumping, you'll need to slow down. Feel free to start early.

49

Practice in front of a video camera.

We're now moving into the phase of "Olympic Presentations," where only the strong survive. Tape yourself presenting in front of a video camera. You don't have to tape the entire presentation—just the relevant parts. Recognize that most of us become a bit nervous when a video camera is shoved in front of our faces, so don't be too hard on yourself when you view the video the first time.

Make notes and identify what needs to change.

Videos, both fortunately and unfortunately, provide you with a ton of data. This is one of the reasons we advocate only videotaping a portion of your presentation, then going back and videotaping more. As you focus on one piece at a time, you can address a smaller number of concerns at a time as opposed to attempting to address everything that might bother you about your presentation.

51

Pay close attention to the use of your body.

Most of us don't pay much attention to our bodies. We tend to drag them along from event to event as if they are prisoners of ours. Consistent with that, we don't often pay attention to the messages that our bodies might be sending that are contrary to the messages that emerge from our mouths. As you look at your videotape, do you find consistency between "the words and the music"? Or are they at odds?

52

Notice how you use your body in space.

Do you appear to be a little wooden man or woman standing in front of your audience? Or are you a pogo stick—hopping from place to place and never appearing to land any place? If so, fix this. As was mentioned in #51, how you use your body also sends a message about the seriousness with which you hold your presentation. As you review your videotape, look for a natural use of the body that does not draw too much attention to itself.

53

Practice in front of live people. Pay them if necessary.

As comfortable as you are in front of a video camera, the presence of live people might change all that. Between their fidgeting, side conversations, cell phone calls, coughing, scratching, and numerous other distractions, you might find yourself disoriented. Rather than waiting until you're in front of a live "for-real" audience, get one of your own and see how it works for you. Let the scratching begin!

54

Practice until you like what you see.

Or, practice until you have run out of time or have become absolutely bored with everything that is contained in your presentation. If your presentation is important (and we assume it is), you won't want to short change the amount of time you put into this preparation phase. It may very well make the difference between "top-of-the-heap" and "bottom-of-the-bag."

Decide if you will use media support.

Most presentations these days use some sort of media support. This is usually in the form of computer-generated slides produced in software programs such as PowerPoint. Media support is a particularly good idea if you're dealing with a large audience because it helps the audience feel more connected to you and what you're saying. Media also provides an additional level of reinforcement of the message that you're presenting.

56

Don't put your entire life history on one slide.

A common mistake many people make in the use of slides is putting so much information on the slide that it is virtually impossible to either see and/or understand. Make sure your slides don't contain an overwhelming amount of information. If necessary, use more slides, but keep them clean in terms of organization.

57

Put only three to five lines on a slide.

This may sound like a paltry amount of information, but keeping the content of your slides to three to five lines allows you to maintain a font size of approximately 32 points. This will make your presentation much more visible from greater distances. This will also help your audience focus on the content rather than the fact that they cannot read the content because of the miniature font size chosen.

58

Incorporate illustrations into your slides.

Graphics are a great addition to your slide as are illustrations or comics from other sources. In some instances, you might need to obtain the author's permission before using these graphics or illustrations. The software that came with your computer, however, might contain illustrations or graphics that you would be able to use without having to obtain the author's permission.

Use animation in your slides—if you are able to.

Animations of a limited nature (which are available through some software packages) add interest to the images on the screen. They can also be distracting, however, so use them judiciously. Bear in mind that the addition of illustrations might increase the number of "clicks" necessary to move to the next slide unless you program your animation to occur automatically.

Run through the flow of your slides.

Far too many executives have their administrative assistants develop their slide decks, then the executives stand up before the audience and run through the slides for the first time audience—having no idea of the flow, or the presence or absence of automation. This is *not* good. Make sure you know the general flow of the presentation and, where necessary, adjust the presentation deck to fit your style and approach—particularly if someone else developed the deck for you.

61

Put your slides in a format you can take with you.

It is common to electronically send presentation decks ahead of time to the location where you're presentating. The positive side of this is you know your presentation is there and it is ready for your delivery. The negative side is you don't know how the receiving computer has adjusted your presentation. If you have a laptop computer, take it with you and ensure your presentation is on it. Or put the presentation on a CD or USB drive.

62

Carry a floppy disk and a CD with you.

This might seem to be akin to wearing both a belt and suspenders, but today's computers do not all have the same options. If you are taking your presentation with you (even if it's on a laptop), you might want to take a floppy disk, a CD, and even a USB storage device (or disk "key") with you. That way you know you have your presentation with you in a usable format.

63

Make memory joggers for yourself.

Although many people use full-sized pages that hold their written-out presentations or speeches, some individuals prefer index cards that contain the main ideas (they fill in the rest on the basis of their memories and preparation). Full-sized pages are much more common with sermons, political speeches, or other more formal business presentations. The use of index cards is more common with less formal talks.

64

Number your memory joggers.

Nothing is quite so frightening as the presenter who puts his or her notes on index cards (or full-sized pages) and fails to number them, only to drop the presentation on the way to speak. The resulting debacle is easily prevented: Number the pages. In addition, you can put a rubber band around index cards until you're ready to use them, or you can three-hole punch full-size pages and put them in a binder.

Practice with your memory joggers.

The goal of using memory joggers is that you will ultimately appear *not* to be using them. As a result, you'll need to practice with them until you appear natural when using them. This might mean using large print on your full-size pages, using double or triple spacing, or highlighting certain words or statistics. You use these memory joggers to make sure you are including the points you regard as most important.

Keep an extra copy of your memory jogger handy.

Inevitably we lose these things. We don't mean to; we just do. For that reason, it is helpful to have back-up memory joggers. If you're using full-size pages, this is easier than if you're hand writing each index card. Regardless, you might want to have a spare—just in case. If you have a spare, be sure to keep it in a different place than the original (e.g., one in your pocket or purse, the other in your briefcase).

Tune Up!

Tuning up refers to making the necessary last-minute checks to ensure that your presentation is well-positioned for success. Everything from the audience to the timing should be reconfirmed. In the list below, check the box next to each statement that reflects your views about tuning up your presentation.

- ☐ I don't usually tune up my presentation.
- ☐ I don't tune up my presentation if I don't have to.
- ☐ Some days I actually consider tuning up my presentation.
- ☐ I don't have "the gift of gab"—but wish I did.
- ☐ I can stand up and "b___ s___" my way through minutes of worthless rhetoric.
- ☐ This is an opportunity for me to practice my spontaneity. Since I know a lot, it should be easy.

☐ I believe there is a lot I know about this topic, and I am looking forward to an opportunity to share some of that knowledge with others. Tuning up might help.

☐ I see myself becoming more effective at delivering presentations with every one that I do.

If you checked any one of the first six boxes, it may be time for you to reconsider your beliefs about tuning up your presentation. As you do and begin to adopt some of the beliefs and assumptions reflected in the last two, you'll enjoy presentations more—and your audience will likely enjoy them more also.

67

Reconfirm your presentation logistics.

As close as possible to the time and day of your presentation, reconfirm the logistics associated with it: The room, the audience size, the time, the media that will be available, and when you might be able to enter the room to set up everything. You might even want to create a form or checklist that will serve as a reminder of the things you need to clarify, review, or confirm.

68

Arrive at your destination early.

Nothing unnerves presenters more than arriving at their destination just in time and having to go "on" immediately. One presenter described it as feeling "shot out of a cannon." Since most human beings would not choose to be shot out of a cannon, start early. You'll feel better and you'll be able to put your best foot forward.

69

Make sure you pack your own "parachute."

By "packing your own parachute," we mean making sure that you are very familiar with all the factors that might affect your presentation. Is there music playing in the room? Are the lights dimmed? Is a lectern missing? Is one there that shouldn't be? Will you have a microphone? Is it on a stand or clipped to your lapel? Is the battery in the lapel microphone a fresh one?

70

Walk around the room—get comfortable.

According to Charles Garfield, author of *Peak Performance,* one of the things that peak performers do is they envision themselves as being successful. As an effective presenter, you will need to do this very thing. If possible, obtain access to the room where you will be presenting. Then walk about the room, imagining yourself presenting effectively to your audience.

71

Breathe.

One of the things that frequently goes first during a stressful (or anticipated stressful) presentation is the presenter's breathing. Don't let that happen to you. Practice deep, belly breaths in the space where you will be presenting. The impact of full breaths on a presenter's overall comfort level is significant. Breathing deeply (five to six breaths should be adequate) helps your body feel more relaxed and focused. Breathing also serves to relieve some of the bodily tension you might be feeling.

72

Say a few words to your (soon-to-be) audience.

Rehearsing the opening words or phrases of your presentation will help your voice settle in initially. This settling-in period should be helpful to you in ensuring that your voice doesn't crack and that the microphone's volume (if you're using a micro-phone) is set at a proper level. Listen carefully to the way you sound. It is often amazing how much the sound of our voices changes based on the set-ting in which we're speaking. Minimize the shock.

73

Have a banana.

Musicians, actors, and other performing artists have found that having a banana before they perform significantly reduces the amount of anxiety they experience. Although there are well-documented physiological reasons for this, suffice it to say that eating a banana helps you deal with the excess adrenaline you might have prior to speaking. For best results, eat the banana two to three hours before you're due to present. You'll likely be amazed at the impact such a simple act can have on the way you feel. Have a banana—maybe even two.

74

Check out your visuals for clarity and impact.

If your presentation incorporates slides, review the slides (at least a few of them) in the room where you'll be presenting. This is particularly important if you're using someone else's computer for the presentation. Depending on the other individual's set of fonts, the fonts in your presentation might have changed and might look like some unknown foreign language. Avoid this potential embarrassment by reviewing your slides—and adjusting the fonts if needed.

75

Meet your audience as they arrive.

Meeting your audience as they arrive allows you to do several things: 1) It makes these individuals seem more like people and less like critics; 2) It gives you something worthwhile to do while you're playing "the waiting game"; and 3) It allows you to check for rotten fruits and vegetables they may have brought.

76

Check your hands for excessive perspiration.

There are few things that are less appealing than shaking hands with a person who seems to have just left a sauna. If you are prone to excess perspiration when you're "on edge," keep a handkerchief, tissue, or paper towel handy so that your nervousness is not obvious to those meeting you prior to your presentation. Hold on to whatever you use; you might need it after the presentation as well.

When You're "On"

You have now come to the culmination point of all your preparation. This is where "the rubber meets the road," the time that "separates the sheep from the goats," and _____ (insert your favorite metaphor here). In the list below, check the box next to each statement that reflects your views about delivering presentations.

☐ I'd just as soon someone deliver the presentation.

☐ I wouldn't give this presentation if I didn't have to.

☐ Some days I'm better at presenting than others.

☐ Wouldn't it just be easier to fake an illness?

☐ I just can't stand up and "b___ s___" my way through minutes of worthless rhetoric. I'm a "just the facts" kind of person.

☐ This is an opportunity for me to impress people with what I know about a given topic.

☐ I believe I've prepared myself well, and believe there is a lot that can be accomplished through this presentation.

☐ I see myself becoming more effective at delivering presentations with every one that I do.

If you checked any one of the first six boxes, it may be time for you to reconsider your beliefs about your presentations. Now that you've prepared, get ready for great results—and a great time.

77

Smile as you're being introduced.

In most presentation settings, you'll be introduced prior to actually speaking. And in many settings, you'll be in full view as you're being introduced. Although it sounds trivial, Smile! The person introducing is doing his or her best to "warm up" the audience prior to you beginning. If you're sitting on the stage looking as if you're about to receive a public root canal, it doesn't help your cause. Smile!

78

See #71.

During the "tune up" section, you were instructed to practice breathing. Try it again at this point. Breathing will help you become grounded in your presentation and will enable you to be more "present" for your audience's sake and for your own. As you did in #71, practice a deep belly breath, allowing your stomach to extend and your abdomen to take in its full capacity of air. As you experienced previously, it will serve you well in reducing tension and in helping to set your focus on the task at hand.

79

Thank the person who introduced you.

This is generally considered polite. It's not a mandate, but people will think you have a level of manners if you at least acknowledge the person who introduced you. If you're intellectually quick and can come up with a humorous self-effacing remark (such as, "With all those great words, I was wondering if someone was going to speak before me!"), you will help your audience feel at ease—and you will as well.

80

Look at them.

They won't bite. And even if they will, you should be far enough away from them that you'll have a head start for the exit. Looking directly at the audience as you begin also sends a statement that says, "I'm not afraid of you." It lets the audience know that you see them and that you're interested in establishing a dialogue with them. If you look at them and smile, you may have won additional "warmth" points for yourself. And you will feel better about them—just as they will feel better about you.

81

Begin speaking with great confidence.

Do the best you can to keep your "great confidence" from sounding like shouting, berating, or any other negative response. Instead, speak clearly, comfortably, and with ease. If you need to, remain close to the lectern at the beginning of your presentation. This may help you feel a bit more comfortable in the setting. And you'll be able to be reasonably close to your notes.

82

Establish eye contact around the room.

Each audience member has come to hear you. For that reason, it is best when you are able to establish eye contact with every person in the room. Do not allow your eye contact to be quick and fleeting, but instead look at the audience members for a few seconds prior to moving on to look at a different audience member. As you establish eye contact, audience members feel as if you're speaking directly to them. And you are.

83

Stay in touch with your memory joggers.

Most people practice the beginning of their presentations far more often than they do either the middle or the end. If you have done this, you might begin with a false sense of confidence relative to how much of your presentation you have memorized. Staying in touch with your memory joggers (index cards or full-page printouts) allows you to lean on them when necessary.

84

Move about the room as you would like.

Unless you're being videotaped or are positioning yourself so that hearing-impaired members of the audience can lip read your message, there's no significant reason for locking yourself in one particular place. Establish a reasonable radius for yourself (no speaking from the hall, please) within which you can move, and move within that radius. This practice is also useful for keeping your audience awake because they'll have to move their heads to follow you.

85

Keep your hands in plain sight at all times.

The notable exception to this suggestion is when you are reaching for an item that will be used in your presentation. If you are, reach for the item then leave your hands outside of your pockets. It is far too tempting to start juggling the loose change that is in your pocket, or playing with a loose paper clip that you've found.

86

If you naturally gesture, do so.

The use of hands in a presentation could easily be the topic of an entire book, but for our purposes, think of gestures as women often think of makeup. Too much, and you'll start to look like a clown. Too little, and you'll likely fade into the walls. The right amount will add color, interest, and attractiveness to the content of your presentation and to you as the presenter.

87

Face the audience as you speak.

The use of visual aids, slides, and other visual tools might require you to turn in such a way that you can at least notice if they're working properly. If you need to, go ahead, but do not spend more than a few seconds in that direction. If you do, you'll likely find your audience's attention distracted because they see your attention being distracted.

88

Use a laser pointer for emphasis.

Rather than turning your back to the audience to point to something you regard as important, stand to the side and use a laser pointer that significantly extends your reach. This will allow you to point the audience's attention to the particular part of the slide that you deem important while, at the same time, maintain eye contact with them. Some digital projectors come with laser pointers. If yours does, use it.

89

Make your face match your words.

If your presentation is designed to discuss a serious issue, make sure you look serious. If, on the other hand, you're delivering great news and want to encourage the audience to celebrate with you, that will require a different "look." Your purpose should be well-linked to your look. As you hear the words coming out of your mouth, make sure the expressions on your face and the way you are using your body agree.

Make necessary minor changes as you go along.

Once your audience has arrived, you have the ultimate data, which is the people themselves. This "ultimate data" might lead you in a different direction than your original intent. If it doesn't "wig you out" too much, do it. This is particularly true of certain jokes, illustrations, or other attempts at humor. In looking at your audience, you may think that your device (joke, illustration, etc.) might not work. This could be useful data for you. Don't be afraid to use it.

91

Involve your audience as necessary.

Asking your audience questions to which they will either raise their hands, respond verbally (as a group), or respond individually is a great way to get them involved. This breaks the boredom of simply listening to a "talking head" for some stretch of time. If you are able to do this comfortably, do so. Your audience will appreciate the change of activity and any physical movement allows them to stretch.

92

Monitor your time usage carefully.

In most speaking situations, you are provided with time limits for your presentations. Do your best not to violate them; this will greatly facilitate your being invited back again in the future. Usually there is a clock on the wall of the room where you're presenting (check it for accuracy if there is). If there is no clock, use your own watch, or ask someone in the group to give you a sign when your available time has diminished to five or ten minutes. You'll be glad they did.

93

Follow your plan diligently.

Some more daring speakers like to improvise their presentations as they go along. If this is your "thing," then this book is probably of limited value to you except for this advice: Don't. Improvisation, unless you are highly skilled at it, seldom produces the quality of outcome that a well-thought-out and well-delivered presentation does. If you have great experience and want to change, do so at your own risk.

94

When you are finished, stop and sit down.

Some speakers are like children who, although they have learned how to ride a bicycle, have not learned how to stop. As in the case of children, this inability to stop can create some uncomfortable disasters. If your presentation is finished, thank the audience and sit. If it's not and your time is up, review the key points that you've covered, thank the audience, and sit down.

Be Your Own Biggest Fan

You survived it! Congratulations. But, your learning about presentations is not quite finished. In the list below, check the box next to each statement that reflects your views about your after-presentation activities.

☐ I'd just as soon take a nap as talk about my presentation.

☐ I don't particularly want to go over my presentation again.

☐ Some days I think about my presentation.

☐ Wouldn't it just be easier to fake an illness?

☐ Having "b___ s___"ed my way through this presentation, I'm one step closer to doing the same for its successor.

☐ I just hope the audience walked away impressed—since that was really what I was going after.

☐ I believe I've prepared myself well and believe that the delivery went well, but I know
there are probably some things I could have
done better.

☐ I want to get better and better at this, and I
know that getting better will probably require me to look at my "game tapes."

This first phase of follow up allows you to com-
mend yourself for those things that went well.
Subsequent levels of follow up will look at the
other things you might want to consider for future
presentations. For now, however, we will focus
only on the good stuff.

95

Congratulate yourself on the things done well.

Chances are, you did a number of things in your presentation that were just great. It might have been the joke you told, the clarity of the slides you used, or your overall comfort with the presentation. Whatever you did that you believe contributed to the success of your presentation, write it down. Capitalize on these successes as you undertake future presentations. Focus only on the good!

96

Listen for kudos in the feedback from others.

In many settings, audience members will approach you after the presentation to share their appreciation for your presentation. What are they saying? What did they like most? What did they find most valuable about the content? The delivery? Often, you will not have to prompt them for this information; they'll tell you. When they do, make mental or physical notes for your future reference.

Unearth the Bad News

Having focused on the positive, successful parts of your presentation, you'll now focus on those things that could have gone better. These might not have all been awful; they might have simply been less than what you wanted. In the list below, check the box next to each statement that reflects your views about your after-presentation activities:

☐ I'd just as soon take a nap as review the negative aspects of my presentation.

☐ I don't particularly want to go over my presentation.

☐ Some days I think about this—and only this.

☐ I think I *am* sick.

☐ At this point, I have a well-crafted fantasy of my overall adequacy. Please don't ruin it.

☐ I just hope the audience went away—someday I'll figure this "improvement" stuff out.

☐ I believe I've prepared myself well and believe that the delivery went well, but I know there are probably some things I could have done better.

☐ I want to get better and better at this, and I know that getting better will probably require me to look at my "game tapes."

The second phase of follow up allows you to identify the improvement areas of your presentation. Just as we focused only on the things that went well in the previous section, we'll focus only on the improvements here.

97

Identify the things that didn't go so well.

Just as you were challenged to be generous with your praises in the previous section, be equally generous with your areas for improvement. As you did before, just make a list of the things that didn't come off as well as you would have liked. Don't engage in deep analysis of the reasons for these issues, just list them for now. We'll analyze and "buff them up" in the next section.

98

Listen for improvements in others' feedback.

Most people do not share their criticism—constructive or otherwise—with the speaker. They tend to share it with each other. If someone offers you suggestions for improvement, thank them graciously and write down the improvement. Even if you don't' agree with it, write it down. There will be opportunities to explore it and determine what to do with it later.

Fall in Love with Japanese

The Japanese have a wonderful word that seems appropriate in this last section of our consideration of effective presentations. That word is kaizen, meaning "continual improvement." Unless you are already a brilliant speaker, you might have noticed some areas where you can improve. Don't let this learning evaporate. In the list below, check the box next to each statement that reflects your views about continual improvement.

☐ I'm largely hopeless.
☐ I don't particularly want to go over my presentation again.
☐ I might dig out my presentation at some point, but not now.
☐ How can you improve on perfection?

☐ At this point, I have a well-crafted fantasy of my overall adequacy. More data will only ruin it.

☐ I probably have too much to improve—and too little time to deal with this.

☐ I believe I can improve and am committed to doing so.

☐ I had better get started. Otherwise I might forget the lessons that this presentation brought me.

Your final thoughts are captured in the remaining three activities. As you execute these you will find that you'll get better and better, and you'll help others to get better as well.

Write down specific things to do differently.

Rather than tossing out generalities and hoping that there is a sufficient amount of information in these to help you improve, *be specific*. Rather than saying something like "Use fewer slides," say, "Use no more than 40 slides for a presentation of this length." The second improvement is far more actionable than the first one.

100

File away your improvements for reference.

Most of us will have numerous opportunities to improve our presentations—whether we want them or not. Yet for many of us, we do not present daily, weekly, or even monthly. It happens occasionally and, because of that, it might be possible to forget the things we want to improve. We might also forget the things we've done well that we simply want to repeat. Create a list of both items for yourself. Make a "presentation file" for future reference. Then use it.

101

Give a copy of this book to a friend.

If you've followed even a few of the suggestions listed here, you will likely have noticed a significant improvement both in the quality and the comfort of your presentations.

There are a number of folks out there like you, by the way, who could also use these suggestions to help them improve. You've likely written in the margins of this book, or it is pretty ratty from your active use of it.

So why not purchase copies of this book for those with whom you interact who could use the

thoughts here to become even more effective presenters?

You can purchase copies of our books on the Web
by accessing our Website, www.HRDPress.com.
There you can also learn about our other *101
Leadership Actions* books that will be useful in significantly improving the quality of your life and
the quality of your work.

We wish you every success as you grow person-
ally and professionally.